Samsung Galaxy S24 Ultra

VS
iPhone 15 Pro Max
Ultimate Camera and Performance Showdown

Unveiling the Clash of Titans - A Comprehensive Comparison of the Flagship Giants in 2024

Tech Talker

Table of contents

Introduction

In the ever-evolving realm of technology, innovations unfold at a relentless pace, shaping the way we live, work, and connect. The fast-paced tech industry, a dynamic landscape driven by constant advancements, thrives on the ceaseless quest for innovation. Companies engage in a relentless race, pushing the boundaries of what is possible and redefining the benchmarks of excellence. This overview sets the stage for a journey through the transformative developments that have taken place in the tech world, capturing the essence of an industry that never sleeps.

In the vast expanse of the tech cosmos, few events generate ripples as profound as the Galaxy AI event—an annual spectacle that propels the digital realm into unprecedented dimensions. The year was marked by palpable anticipation, with tech enthusiasts and aficionados eagerly awaiting the unveiling of the Samsung Galaxy S24 Series. The event wasn't just a showcase; it was a rendezvous with the future, a glimpse into the technological marvels that would soon be at our fingertips.

As the curtains parted at the Galaxy AI event, the collective breaths held in suspense were released in a crescendo of excitement. The star of the show, the Samsung Galaxy S24 Ultra, took center stage, casting its brilliance across the tech landscape. The event's significance lay not merely in the unveiling of a new smartphone but in the orchestration of innovation, a convergence of cutting-edge technology and avant-garde design.

The anticipation leading up to this moment was akin to the hushed whispers before the opening act of a grand performance. Enthusiasts speculated about the features, the design, and the technological leaps that Samsung would introduce. The Galaxy AI event, like a digital overture, set the stage for the unveiling, promising a symphony of advancements that would echo in the corridors of the tech world.

In this narrative, we embark on a journey not just to compare two flagship smartphones—the Samsung Galaxy S24 Ultra and the iPhone 15 Pro Max—but to unravel the narrative spun at the Galaxy AI event. It's a tale of anticipation, innovation, and the relentless pursuit of excellence, as these technological giants vie for the throne in the ever-evolving saga of smartphone supremacy.

Chapter 1:

The Unveiling

The Galaxy AI event wasn't merely an exhibition; it was a seismic event that sent shockwaves through the tech community. As the doors of anticipation swung open, attendees and virtual spectators found themselves thrust into a realm where innovation danced hand in hand with imagination. The event was a pilgrimage for tech enthusiasts, a sacred ground where the future unfolded pixel by pixel.

At the heart of the spectacle was the Samsung Galaxy S24 Ultra, a beacon of technological prowess that drew the spotlight with an intensity akin to a celestial body. The event showcased not just a product launch but a manifesto—an affirmation that the future had arrived, clad in metal and glass, powered by the relentless march of innovation.

The impact of the Galaxy AI event rippled through the tech community, leaving an indelible mark on the collective consciousness of enthusiasts, developers, and competitors alike. It wasn't just about the unveiling of a new smartphone series; it was a declaration of Samsung's commitment to pushing the boundaries of what's possible.

Tech forums buzzed with discussions, social media channels became virtual amphitheaters for dissecting every feature, and online communities resonated with the hum of excitement. The Galaxy AI event sparked debates, fueled speculation, and, most importantly, ignited the flames of anticipation that burned in the hearts of tech enthusiasts around the globe.

In the aftermath of the event, the impact lingered like the echo of a resounding chord. Developers were inspired to explore the newfound capabilities, competitors recalibrated their strategies, and consumers found themselves at the cusp of a technological crossroads. The Galaxy AI event wasn't just a moment in time; it was a catalyst for change, a ripple that would shape the trajectory of the tech industry for the foreseeable future.

As we delve into the intricacies of the Samsung Galaxy S24 Ultra and the iPhone 15 Pro Max, it's crucial to understand the backdrop against which these devices emerged. The Galaxy AI event wasn't a mere showcase; it was a cultural phenomenon, an ode to innovation that resonated far beyond the confines of convention halls and virtual stages. It was the spark that ignited a technological revolution, and the repercussions of its brilliance continue to illuminate the path ahead.

The features and specifications of the Samsung Galaxy s24 Ultra

In the ever-evolving landscape of smartphones, the Samsung Galaxy S24 Ultra emerges as a colossus, a device that encapsulates the zenith of technological achievement. Let's embark on a journey through its features and specifications, dissecting the intricacies that set it apart in the crowded galaxy of flagship smartphones.

Display Extravaganza:

The centerpiece of the Galaxy S24 Ultra is undoubtedly its expansive 6.8-inch QHD+ Dynamic AMOLED 2X display. With a resolution of 3120 by 1440 pixels, this visual masterpiece breathes life into every pixel, creating a canvas where colors pop with vibrancy, and details emerge with stunning clarity. The decision to adopt a flat display this year is a nod to practicality, departing from the curved trend of yesteryears. This isn't just a screen; it's a portal to a visual realm enhanced by a fast 120Hz refresh rate and HDR10+ support. With a peak brightness of 2500 nits, outdoor visibility is elevated to new heights.

A Performance Powerhouse:

Under the hood, the Galaxy S24 Ultra is a juggernaut, powered by the Snapdragon 8 Gen 3 chipset. This 4nm arm-based powerhouse flexes its muscles with a single core of the latest arm Cortex X4-based Prime core, clocked at up to 3.3 GHz. The performance benchmarks dance in harmony with the S Pen, showcasing not just raw power but a symphony of efficiency. It's a performance ballet where the Galaxy S24 Ultra and the Snapdragon 8 Gen 3 waltz close to the heels of their competitors, making a compelling case for technological supremacy.

Optical Symphony - Camera System:

The camera system of the Galaxy S24 Ultra is a testament to Samsung's relentless pursuit of photographic excellence. A formidable quad rear camera setup headlines with a staggering 200-megapixel primary sensor, adorned with optical image stabilization (OIS) and an f/1.7 aperture. The dual telephoto setup is a spectacle in itself, featuring a 50-megapixel quad-pixel autofocus sensor with OIS, offering 5x optical zoom, and a 10-megapixel sensor with 3x optical zoom. Completing the quartet is a 12-megapixel ultrawide-angle sensor, providing a panoramic 120° field of view. The selfie realm isn't overlooked, with a 12-megapixel front sensor capturing the nuances of self-expression.

Endurance Redefined:

Beneath the sleek exterior lies a robust 5000mAh battery, an encore performance from its predecessor. While the battery capacity remains consistent, the Snapdragon 8 Gen 3 chipset brings forth a new cadence to the power symphony. Charging speeds, however, continue to be an arena where Samsung strides with confidence, offering 45 Watts of fast charging. The Galaxy S24 Ultra deftly balances the equation between power and efficiency, ensuring that the device doesn't merely endure but thrives in the marathon of daily usage.

Software Ecosystem:

Beyond the tangible hardware, the Galaxy S24 Ultra extends an olive branch to the future with a promise of software support that transcends the ordinary. Samsung, in a paradigm-shifting move, pledges 7 years of software updates for the Galaxy S24 Ultra. This commitment, coupled with the intuitive One UI, transforms the device into a timeless companion in the ever-evolving tech landscape.

The Samsung Galaxy S24 Ultra isn't just a smartphone; it's an odyssey into the frontiers of technology. It's a manifestation of innovation, a symphony of pixels, and a testament to Samsung's unwavering commitment to redefining the boundaries of what a flagship device can achieve. As we navigate the labyrinth of its features, it becomes evident that the Galaxy S24 Ultra isn't a device bound by the present; it's a herald of the future.

A comparison with the iPhone 15 Pro Max to set the stage for the rivalry

As the curtain rises on the technological stage, it's only fitting to set the scene for a gripping rivalry that transcends the boundaries of brand allegiance. In the spotlight, we have the Samsung Galaxy S24 Ultra, a beacon of innovation, ready to square off against the iPhone 15 Pro Max, Apple's paragon of excellence. The Galaxy S24 Ultra's entrance is marked by the crescendo of the Galaxy AI event, while the iPhone 15 Pro Max enters with the quiet confidence that comes with the Apple legacy.

Display Duel:

The prologue unfolds with a clash of displays, where the Galaxy S24 Ultra brandishes a 6.8-inch QHD+ Dynamic AMOLED 2X spectacle against the iPhone 15 Pro Max's slightly smaller 6.7-inch LTPO Super Retina XDR OLED canvas. The Galaxy's QHD+ resolution at 3120 by 1440 pixels offers a visual symphony, while the iPhone 15 Pro Max, with its 1290 by 2796 pixels, crafts a visual sonnet of its own. The Galaxy, with a flat display, challenges the curved trend, promising not just aesthetics but practicality. The peak brightness of the Galaxy at 2500 nits outshines the iPhone's 2000 nits, setting the stage for a display duel where every pixel contends for supremacy.

Performance Showdown:

The Galaxy S24 Ultra, propelled by the Snapdragon 8 Gen 3 chipset, takes center stage against the iPhone 15 Pro Max's A17 Pro processor. The Snapdragon 8 Gen 3, with its 4nm arm-based architecture, dances on the edge of performance excellence. Meanwhile, Apple, with its A17 Pro, leans on the legacy of crafting custom cores, a tradition that has placed it at the zenith of single-core performance. The numbers on the benchmarks create an overture of competition, with the Galaxy S24 Ultra closing in on the iPhone 15 Pro Max's heels, leaving the audience in suspense over which symphony will echo louder in the realm of performance.

Camera Clash:

The saga unfolds in the photographic realm, where the Galaxy S24 Ultra's quad-camera setup confronts the iPhone 15 Pro Max's triple-camera ensemble. Samsung's photographic opus boasts a 200-megapixel primary sensor, a dual telephoto setup with 5x and 3x optical zoom, and a 12-megapixel ultrawide sensor. The iPhone counters with a 48-megapixel wide-angle sensor, a 12-megapixel ultra-wide, and a 12-megapixel periscope telephoto with 5x optical zoom. The Galaxy's camera repertoire, enriched with features like Nidography Zoom, AI multiframe processing, and deep learning-based super resolution, casts a shadow over the iPhone's photographic prowess.

Endurance and Ecosystem:

In the realm of endurance, the Galaxy S24 Ultra flaunts its 5000mAh battery against the iPhone 15 Pro Max's 4441mAh, promising a symphony of longevity. Charging speeds become a tempo in the narrative, with the Galaxy's 45 Watts fast charging challenging the iPhone's 30 Watts. The grand finale of this comparison unfolds in the software ecosystem, where Samsung's unprecedented pledge of 7 years of software updates for the Galaxy S24 Ultra confronts Apple's legacy of seamless updates and software support.

As the curtain descends on this preliminary comparison, the stage is set for an epic clash between two titans. The Samsung Galaxy S24 Ultra and the iPhone 15 Pro Max, each armed with their technological arsenals, await the final act where consumers will cast their votes, determining the crescendo of this symphony of smartphones.

Chapter 2:

Display Duel

In-depth analysis of the display specifications of both smartphones

The stage is set, and the spotlight shines brightly on the display prowess of two technological titans – the Samsung Galaxy S24 Ultra and the iPhone 15 Pro Max. In this act, we dissect the intricate details of their display specifications, exploring the nuances that define the visual symphony each smartphone orchestrates.

Samsung Galaxy S24 Ultra's Visual Odyssey: The Galaxy S24 Ultra takes the audience on a visual odyssey with its expansive 6.8-inch QHD+ Dynamic AMOLED 2X display. This technological canvas boasts a resolution of 3120 by 1440 pixels, crafting a visual masterpiece that dazzles with clarity and detail. The marriage of quantum dots and organic LEDs in the Dynamic AMOLED 2X display paints each pixel with vibrant colors, deep blacks, and an immersive contrast ratio.

The decision to embrace a flat display marks a departure from the curved trends of yesteryears. Samsung, in its design ethos, not only seeks aesthetics but practicality. This flat canvas reduces the likelihood of accidental touches on the edges and enhances the overall durability of the device. The peak brightness, reaching an impressive 2500 nits, ensures outdoor visibility that rivals the brilliance of a summer day.

The visual symphony doesn't end there. The 120Hz refresh rate, coupled with HDR10+

support, elevates the viewing experience to cinematic levels. Whether it's scrolling through content, gaming, or watching high-definition videos, the Galaxy S24 Ultra's display is a symphony of seamless motion and dynamic color.

iPhone 15 Pro Max's Visual Sonnet: In response to the Galaxy's symphony, the iPhone 15 Pro Max presents its visual sonnet on a slightly smaller 6.7-inch LTPO Super Retina XDR OLED stage. The resolution, at 1290 by 2796 pixels, may be lower than its competitor, but Apple, with its meticulous calibration, ensures a visual feast that captivates the audience.

The LTPO (Low-Temperature Polycrystalline Oxide) technology in the

Super Retina XDR OLED display enables dynamic refresh rates, conserving power when high refresh rates are unnecessary. The 120Hz refresh rate harmonizes with the Pro Motion technology, delivering fluid interactions and scrolling.

While the peak brightness of 2000 nits falls slightly short of the Galaxy's radiance, the Ceramic Shield on top of the display adds a layer of durability, enhancing drop performance. The visual sonnet of the iPhone's display, characterized by accurate color reproduction and deep blacks, invites users into a world where every pixel is finely tuned.

A Comparative Glimpse: As the act concludes, a comparative glimpse reveals the strengths and nuances of each display. The Galaxy S24 Ultra, with its larger canvas, higher resolution, and impressive brightness, commands attention in the visual symphony. The decision to opt for a flat display and the adoption of HDR10+ support further solidify its position.

On the other hand, the iPhone 15 Pro Max, in its visual sonnet, relies on meticulous calibration, LTPO technology, and the durability-enhancing Ceramic Shield. While the peak brightness may be slightly dimmer, Apple's commitment to color accuracy and the Pro Motion technology enrich the visual experience.

In this display duel, each smartphone presents a unique visual narrative, leaving consumers to choose the symphony that resonates most profoundly with their preferences. The curtain falls, but the echoes of this visual clash linger, setting the stage for the next act in the smartphone symphony.

In the grand tapestry of smartphone displays, the Samsung Galaxy S24 Ultra stands as a masterpiece, and at the heart of this visual spectacle is its QHD+ Dynamic AMOLED 2X display. As the curtains rise, let's delve into the brilliance of this technological canvas, a symphony of pixels that redefine what users can expect from a visual experience.

At the core of the Galaxy S24 Ultra's display prowess is its Quantum High Definition Plus

(QHD+) resolution. With a staggering 3120 by 1440 pixels, this display transcends the boundaries of conventional clarity. Every pixel becomes a brushstroke in the artist's hand, painting images with meticulous detail and unrivaled sharpness.

The impact of QHD+ is most palpable in day-to-day activities, from scrolling through text to immersing oneself in multimedia content. Texts become crisper, images more lifelike, and videos a journey into high-definition realms. The canvas, with over four million pixels, is a playground for visual perfection.

As the audience marvels at the visuals, the Dynamic AMOLED 2X technology takes center stage, orchestrating a symphony of colors that dance across the screen. The marriage of quantum dots and organic LEDs breathes life into each hue, producing a spectrum that's as vibrant as the artist's palette.

Deep blacks become an abyss of richness, providing a stark contrast to the brilliance of colors. The high dynamic range (HDR) capabilities elevate the viewing experience, ensuring that shadows and highlights are not just seen but felt. Whether it's the subtlety of a sunset or the explosion of fireworks, the Dynamic AMOLED 2X display renders each moment with breathtaking authenticity.

In a departure from the curved trends, Samsung opts for practical elegance by embracing a flat display. This decision isn't merely aesthetic; it's a commitment to user experience. Accidental touches on the edges are minimized, providing a canvas that responds precisely to the user's intentions.

The flat brilliance doesn't compromise on style; it enhances it. The sleek lines of the Galaxy S24 Ultra, combined with the flat display, create a device that's not just a technological marvel but a design statement. It's a marriage of form and function, where every curve – or lack thereof – tells a story of thoughtful design.

As the crescendo builds, the Galaxy S24 Ultra unveils its trump card – a peak brightness of 2500 nits. This isn't just a number; it's a proclamation of outdoor visibility that defies the sun itself. The display becomes a beacon, cutting through the glare of the midday sun and ensuring that every detail remains crystal clear.

Whether you're checking your phone under the bright sky or editing photos on a sunny day, the Galaxy S24 Ultra's display stands resolute, ensuring that you don't miss a single nuance. The radiance extends beyond mere numbers; it's a commitment to a visual experience that transcends environmental challenges.

In the grand narrative of smartphone displays, the QHD+ Dynamic AMOLED 2X display in the Galaxy S24 Ultra emerges not just as a feature but as the protagonist. It's a canvas that goes beyond imagination, a symphony of pixels that invites users into a world where every detail matters. As the curtain falls on this exploration, the echoes of brilliance linger, setting the Galaxy S24 Ultra apart in the smartphone display symphony.

Comparison of peak brightness, resolution, and display technologies

In the coliseum of smartphone displays, the battle for supremacy unfolds between the Samsung Galaxy S24 Ultra and the iPhone 15 Pro Max. The clash is not just about size but about the very essence of visual brilliance. Let's dissect the key elements – peak brightness, resolution, and display technologies – that define the victor in this epic rivalry.

1. Peak Brightness: A Battle for Visibility

Galaxy S24 Ultra: 2500 Nits vs. iPhone 15 Pro Max: 2000 Nits

The arena is illuminated by the peak brightness of these titans. The Galaxy S24 Ultra steps into the spotlight with an astounding 2500 nits, a luminance that pierces through the brightest of days. Its challenger, the iPhone 15 Pro Max, boasts a commendable 2000 nits, a formidable display of radiance. In the realm of visibility, the Galaxy S24 Ultra takes the lead, ensuring that users bask in the glory of clarity even under the harsh sun.

2. Resolution: The Quest for Pixel Perfection

Galaxy S24 Ultra: 3120x1440 Pixels vs. iPhone 15 Pro Max: 1290x2796 Pixels

As the dust settles, the battlefield reveals the resolution war. The Galaxy S24 Ultra wields a QHD+ resolution, a staggering 3120 by 1440 pixels. Each pixel becomes a soldier in the army of clarity, ensuring that every detail is etched with precision. On the opposing front, the iPhone 15 Pro Max, with 1290 by 2796 pixels, fights valiantly but falls short in the pixel density war. The Galaxy S24 Ultra emerges victorious in the quest for pixel perfection, providing users with a canvas that transcends conventional clarity.

3. Display Technologies: Dynamic AMOLED 2X vs. Super Retina XDR OLED

Galaxy S24 Ultra: Dynamic AMOLED 2X vs. iPhone 15 Pro Max: Super Retina XDR OLED

The heartbeat of these displays is orchestrated by cutting-edge technologies. The Galaxy S24 Ultra boasts Dynamic AMOLED 2X, a symphony of quantum dots and organic LEDs that breathe life into every hue. It's a display that dances with vibrant colors and deep blacks, creating a visual masterpiece. On the opposing side, the iPhone 15 Pro Max flaunts Super Retina XDR OLED, a technology known for its prowess in delivering true blacks and high dynamic range. The battle of technologies is fierce, but the Dynamic AMOLED 2X in the Galaxy S24 Ultra emerges as the maestro, painting a canvas that goes beyond visual imagination.

In the realm of peak brightness, resolution, and display technologies, the Galaxy S24 Ultra stands tall, a beacon of radiance and pixel perfection. The iPhone 15 Pro Max, while a formidable contender, yields to the sheer brilliance and clarity that the Galaxy S24 Ultra brings to the forefront. As the dust settles and the echoes of this display duel linger, one thing is clear – the Galaxy S24 Ultra has set a new standard in the art of visual storytelling.

Chapter 3:

Design Wars

In the enchanting realm of smartphone aesthetics, the Galaxy S24 Ultra and iPhone 15 Pro Max step onto the runway as the epitomes of design elegance. Each silhouette, each curve, and each contour narrates a story of craftsmanship and innovation. Let's delve into the design aspects of these technological marvels and unravel the essence of their visual allure.

The design philosophy echoes in the physicality of these devices. The Galaxy S24 Ultra embraces a boxy demeanor, an embodiment of geometric precision. Every edge, every corner speaks of a calculated poise that not only exudes modernity but also ensures a firm grip. On the opposing end, the iPhone 15 Pro Max takes a different dance with design, its edges caressing the palms with curvaceous charm. The circular embrace of the iPhone 15 Pro Max renders it easy to hold, a testament to ergonomic finesse. In the symphony of form, it's a matter of preference – the poised boxiness of the Galaxy S24 Ultra or the gentle curves of the iPhone 15 Pro Max.

As these titans stand side by side, a keen observer will notice the echoes of their predecessors. The Galaxy S24 Ultra and iPhone 15 Pro Max, with stoic determination, retain the aesthetic DNA that defines their lineages. Evolutionary rather than revolutionary, the design continuity is a nod to the timeless elements that users have grown to love. The Galaxy S24 Ultra and iPhone 15 Pro Max, despite the ever-changing tech landscape, stand as familiar faces, rooted in the design languages that have become iconic.

In the hands of users, the weight of a device becomes a tactile narrative. The Galaxy S24 Ultra, at 232g, possesses a substantial heft, a testament to its robust build and expansive form. On the other end of the spectrum, the iPhone 15 Pro Max graces the palm with 221g of elegance, a lighter touch without compromising on the premium feel. The weight of presence becomes a personal preference – the solid grounding of the Galaxy S24 Ultra or the feather-light allure of the iPhone 15 Pro Max.

In the grand tapestry of design, the Galaxy S24 Ultra and iPhone 15 Pro Max present themselves as canvases where artistry meets functionality. The boxy poise of the Galaxy S24 Ultra and the curvaceous charm of the iPhone 15 Pro Max become brushstrokes, painting a picture of design elegance that caters to diverse sensibilities. As users hold these devices, they don't just hold gadgets; they cradle the result of meticulous design thinking and the legacy of iconic aesthetics.

In the perpetual debate of design aesthetics, the Galaxy S24 Ultra's boxed precision and the iPhone 15 Pro Max's curvaceous comfort emerge as contrasting paradigms, each catering to distinct design sensibilities.

For aficionados of geometric finesse and modernistic elegance, the Galaxy S24 Ultra stands as a paragon of boxed precision. The sharp edges and defined corners encapsulate a design philosophy that speaks of calculated poise. Holding the Galaxy S24 Ultra is like grasping a technological monolith, a device crafted with the meticulousness of a sculptor shaping marble. The boxed precision not only exudes a contemporary aesthetic but also ensures a firm grip, a device meant to be confidently held.

On the flip side of the design spectrum, the iPhone 15 Pro Max invites users into a world of curvaceous comfort. The circular edges of the device, like the embrace of a gentle curve, redefine the tactile experience. It's not just a smartphone; it's a seamlessly integrated extension of the hand. The curvaceous charm of the iPhone 15 Pro Max transcends mere aesthetics; it's about ergonomic finesse. The device nestles comfortably in the palm, its contours aligning with the organic curves of the human hand.

As users navigate the landscape of design preferences, the choice between the Galaxy S24 Ultra and iPhone 15 Pro Max becomes a matter of personal expression. Do you gravitate towards the bold, unapologetic lines of boxed precision, symbolizing a forward-looking aesthetic? Or does the allure of curvaceous comfort, cradling a device that feels like a natural extension of oneself, beckon to your design sensibilities?

In the realm of smartphones, design is not merely a visual facet; it's a tactile and emotional experience. The Galaxy S24 Ultra and iPhone 15 Pro Max, with their design dichotomy, offer users not just gadgets but canvases for self-expression. Whether it's the boxed precision of the Galaxy S24 Ultra or the curvaceous comfort of the iPhone 15 Pro Max, the choice transcends specifications – it becomes a statement of personal style and the embodiment of how one wishes to engage with technology.

The weight and feel of both smartphones in hand

In the realm of smartphones, the dichotomy between weight and feel is a delicate dance, a dance performed differently by the Samsung Galaxy S24 Ultra and the iPhone 15 Pro Max. As users delve into the tangible aspects of these devices, nuances in weight distribution and tactile feedback come to the fore.

Weighing in at 232 grams, the Galaxy S24 Ultra doesn't shy away from presenting a substantial heft. Yet, this weight is not arbitrary; it's a deliberate orchestration of materials and components. The device's weight exudes a sense of sturdiness, a robustness that aligns with its boxed precision design. When cradled in the palm, the Galaxy S24 Ultra feels like a premium entity, an amalgamation of metal and glass engineered for durability. The weight, far from being cumbersome, imparts a reassuring solidity to the device.

Contrasting this, the iPhone 15 Pro Max, though slightly lighter at 221 grams, doesn't compromise on the sense of substance. The weight is distributed meticulously, creating a device that feels substantial without being burdensome. The circular edges contribute to an ergonomic balance, making the iPhone 15 Pro Max an exemplar of balanced ergonomics. Holding it is not just about the weight; it's about an equilibrium that ensures prolonged usage remains comfortable.

Beyond the numerical disparity in grams, the tactile sensation of holding these devices is where the user experience is defined. The Galaxy S24 Ultra, with its boxy contours, offers edges that align confidently with the hand's grasp. It's a device meant to be wielded with purpose, each touchpoint a deliberate engagement with technology.

On the other hand, the iPhone 15 Pro Max, with its circular edges, presents a tactile symphony. The curves nestle seamlessly in the hand, creating an intimate connection. The device becomes an extension of the user, a testament to Apple's pursuit of harmonizing form and function.

Ultimately, the choice between the Galaxy S24 Ultra and iPhone 15 Pro Max in the realm of weight and feel transcends numerical values. It becomes a question of personal preference – do you gravitate towards the intentional heft of boxed precision or the balanced ergonomics of curvaceous comfort? The weight and feel, woven into the fabric of user interaction, contribute to the overarching narrative of how these smartphones seamlessly integrate into the user's daily life.

Chapter 4:

Power Play

The beating heart of any flagship smartphone lies within its chipset, orchestrating a symphony of operations that define the user experience. In the clash of titans – the Samsung Galaxy S24 Ultra and the iPhone 15 Pro Max – the Snapdragon 8 Gen 3 and A17 Pro chipsets take center stage, each boasting its prowess in the relentless pursuit of performance.

At the heart of the Galaxy S24 Ultra resides the Snapdragon 8 Gen 3, a testament to Qualcomm's relentless innovation in the realm of mobile processors. Built on the 4M arm-based architecture, this chipset unveils a single core of the latest arm Cortex X4-based Prime core, clocked at a staggering 3.3 GHz. The Snapdragon 8 Gen 3 is not merely a processor; it's a technological marvel, a powerhouse that propels the Galaxy S24 Ultra into the echelons of cutting-edge performance.

In the opposing corner, the iPhone 15 Pro Max houses the A17 Pro chipset, a creation borne out of Apple's architectural symphony. Unlike Qualcomm's reliance on the latest arm Cortex X4 architecture, Apple charts its course by designing proprietary cores based on the arm architecture. This distinction is not merely semantic; it's a testament to Apple's longstanding tradition of being at the forefront of the performance department.

Benchmark enthusiasts crave empirical evidence, and the Snapdragon 8 Gen 3 delivers a performance narrative that inches remarkably close to the A17 Pro. In the realm of single-core performance, where Apple has traditionally held its ground, the A17 Pro maintains a slim 3% lead over its Snapdragon counterpart. This marginal difference accentuates the fierce competition, with both chipsets pushing the boundaries of what's conceivable in mobile processing.

However, the tale takes an intriguing twist when the spotlight shifts to multi-core performance. Here, the Snapdragon 8 Gen 3 emerges from the shadows, surpassing the A17 Pro in a demonstration of multi-threaded prowess. The numbers etched in benchmarks showcase a realm where Qualcomm's engineering acumen propels the Galaxy S24 Ultra to new heights.

In the relentless pursuit of performance, power efficiency is the unsung hero. The A17 Pro, with its mastery over efficiency cores, retains a slender advantage. Yet, the Snapdragon 8 Gen 3's foray into power efficiency, while not eclipsing its Apple counterpart, narrows the chasm. The Galaxy S24 Ultra, with its Snapdragon heartbeat, stands as a testament to the synergy between raw power and meticulous power management.

In the grand tapestry of mobile processors, the Snapdragon 8 Gen 3 and A17 Pro stand as champions, each with its unique cadence. The Galaxy S24 Ultra, propelled by Qualcomm's engineering prowess, holds its ground against the iPhone 15 Pro Max's A17

Pro. The narrative of performance is not a solitary chapter; it's an ongoing saga, where each benchmark, each operation, defines a new zenith in the relentless pursuit of mobile excellence.

Benchmark comparisons

Embarking on the quest for the ultimate smartphone, the journey invariably winds through the intricate landscapes of benchmarks. In the clash of technological titans, the Samsung Galaxy S24 Ultra and the iPhone 15 Pro Max undergo rigorous scrutiny, each benchmark a chapter that unravels the strengths and shadows of these illustrious devices.

Geekbench, the symphony where processors resonate, echoes with the distinctive crescendo of the A17 Pro within the iPhone 15 Pro Max. The single-core performance, a realm where Apple has traditionally wielded a scepter of supremacy, sees the A17 Pro reigning with a commendable lead. The numbers etched in the silicon annals paint a portrait of singular prowess, a testament to Apple's architectural finesse.

As the benchmark sonata transitions to the multicore movement, the Snapdragon 8 Gen 3 orchestrates a flourish that resonates with multi-threaded might. The Galaxy S24 Ultra, powered by Qualcomm's engineering marvel, eclipses its Apple counterpart in the realm of parallel processing. The multicore symphony is not a mere numerical saga; it's a narrative where the Snapdragon's symphonic capabilities take center stage.

In the epic of benchmarks, AnTuTu unfolds as a comprehensive odyssey, weaving together the threads of CPU, GPU, RAM, and UX performance. Here, the Snapdragon 8 Gen 3, with its multidimensional prowess, crafts a saga of technological ascendancy. The Galaxy S24 Ultra charts a course that traverses the peaks of computational might, leaving an indelible mark on the benchmark odyssey.

The GPU ballet, as choreographed by 3DMark, witnesses a delicate dance between the Adreno GPU of the Galaxy S24 Ultra and the Apple-designed GPU within the iPhone 15 Pro Max. The Snapdragon's Adreno, with its graphical finesse, pirouettes through the graphical landscapes, creating a visual spectacle that stands testament to Qualcomm's dedication to immersive experiences.

In the realm of artificial intelligence, the AI Benchmark Odyssey unfolds, navigating the neural horizons of these technological behemoths. The Galaxy S24 Ultra, fortified with AI features, navigates this odyssey with a finesse that transcends mere processing power. It's not just about numbers; it's about the symbiotic dance between hardware and artificial intelligence that defines a new paradigm in smartphone intelligence.

Even in the brilliance of benchmark victories, shadows cast by weaknesses merit acknowledgment. The Galaxy S24 Ultra, despite its triumphs, faces the perennial challenge of power efficiency, a nuanced dance where optimization meets raw power. The iPhone 15 Pro Max, while holding the scepter of single-core supremacy, encounters a symphony where multi-core nuances hint at the unending pursuit of perfection.

As the benchmark symphony continues, each device plays its unique notes, crafting a narrative of strengths and shadows. The Galaxy S24 Ultra and iPhone 15 Pro Max, each a protagonist in this technological saga, redefine benchmarks not as mere numbers but as chapters in the relentless pursuit of mobile excellence. The benchmark odyssey is not a final destination; it's an ongoing journey where each test, each score, shapes the evolving landscape of smartphone prowess.

The power efficiency and overall performance of each device

In the grand tapestry of technological prowess, power efficiency emerges as a pivotal thread, weaving through the daily symphony of smartphone usage. The Samsung Galaxy S24 Ultra and iPhone 15 Pro Max, each a virtuoso in its own right, unfurl a saga where efficiency meets performance.

The Snapdragon 8 Gen 3, a technological maestro within the Galaxy S24 Ultra, orchestrates a ballet that harmonizes raw power with nuanced efficiency. The 4M arm-based chipset, with its cutting-edge architecture, casts a spell where computational might doesn't come at the cost of excessive power consumption. The Galaxy S24 Ultra, a performance virtuoso, waltzes through tasks with a finesse that belies its formidable capabilities.

In the iPhone 15 Pro Max, Apple's A17 Pro processor takes center stage in a single-core sonata that resonates with the brand's tradition of architectural brilliance. The 3M architecture, a testament to Apple's bespoke approach, navigates the intricacies of tasks with a single-core finesse that defines the iPhone experience. The power efficiency, ingrained in Apple's DNA, manifests in a daily symphony where tasks are orchestrated with a grace that extends battery life.

However, even in the brilliance of technological symphonies, shadows cast by power dynamics linger. The Galaxy S24 Ultra, while wielding the Snapdragon 8 Gen 3 with unparalleled might, faces the perennial challenge of optimizing this power for sustained efficiency. The pursuit of raw power, while admirable, demands a delicate dance with power efficiency to ensure a harmonious user experience.

As the benchmark odyssey unfolds, the multicore symphony becomes a balancing act between power and efficiency. The Galaxy S24 Ultra, with its Snapdragon prowess, dances through multitasking scenarios with a flourish, but the shadows of power consumption lurk in the background. The iPhone 15 Pro Max, with its single-core dominance, encounters a nuanced dance where multi-core efficiency beckons a pursuit of balance.

In the ballet of user experience, where daily tasks become choreographed routines, both devices strive to strike a balance. The Galaxy S24 Ultra, with its Snapdragon heartbeat, aims for a seamless performance tapestry where efficiency guides every interaction. The iPhone 15 Pro Max, with its A17 Pro at the helm, crafts a daily symphony where single-core finesse meets the efficiency demands of modern smartphone usage.

In the final movement of this technological symphony, the verdict is one of diversity. The Galaxy S24 Ultra and iPhone 15 Pro Max, each a protagonist in the efficiency narrative, redefine power not as a blunt force but as a nuanced dance. Efficiency becomes the unifying theme, a thread that binds the daily experiences of users in a harmonious blend of power and optimization. The technological saga continues, where each device, in its own way, contributes to the evolving melody of smartphone excellence.

Chapter 5:
Camera Clash

In the realm of smartphone photography, where pixels dance to paint life's vivid tapestry, the Galaxy S24 Ultra and iPhone 15 Pro Max emerge as virtuoso storytellers. Each device, armed with a cadre of lenses, unravels a narrative where visual nuances become an eloquent expression of technological finesse.

The Galaxy S24 Ultra, a photographic maestro, dons a quad-camera symphony that unfolds a visual epic. At the helm is the 200-megapixel primary sensor, a pixel-rich canvas capturing life's minutest details. With optical image stabilization (OIS) and a wide f/1.7 aperture, the primary sensor becomes a virtuoso in low-light scenarios, painting vibrant stories in the canvas of the night.

The dual telephoto setup in the Galaxy S24 Ultra orchestrates duets of optical brilliance. A 50-megapixel quad-pixel autofocus sensor, armed with OIS and 5x optical zoom, becomes a visual maestro in capturing distant tales. Its counterpart, a 10-megapixel sensor with OIS and 3x optical zoom, complements the symphony, adding layers to visual narratives.

The 12-megapixel ultrawide angle sensor in the Galaxy S24 Ultra expands the visual horizon with a 120° field of view. The aperture of f/2.2 becomes a portal to expansive landscapes, capturing the grandeur of scenes with a sweeping panorama. The ultrawide lens, a silent narrator, adds breadth to the visual saga painted by the Galaxy S24 Ultra.

At the forefront of self-portraiture, the Galaxy S24 Ultra features a 12-megapixel selfie sensor with an aperture of f/2.2. This front-facing virtuoso becomes a storyteller of expressions, adding a personal touch to the visual odyssey crafted by the device. In the Galaxy S24 Ultra's camera ensemble, every lens becomes a note in the symphony of visual storytelling.

In the photographic odyssey of the iPhone 15 Pro Max, a triple-camera ensemble emerges as a testament to Apple's commitment to visual excellence. The 48-megapixel wide-angle sensor, adorned with an f/1.8 aperture, captures life's nuances with a finesse that defines the iPhone photography legacy. The primary sensor, a visual conductor, orchestrates scenes with clarity and precision.

The secondary act in the iPhone 15 Pro Max's visual narrative unfolds with a 12-megapixel ultrawide angle sensor boasting an f/2.2 aperture. This lens becomes a portal to expansive vistas, painting scenes with a breadth that complements the primary sensor. Together, the wide and ultrawide lenses in the iPhone 15 Pro Max create a visual tapestry that captures the essence of moments.

The tertiary lens in the iPhone 15 Pro Max's camera triad is a 12-megapixel periscope telephoto sensor. With an f/2.8 aperture and 5x optical zoom, this lens becomes a storyteller of distant details. The periscope telephoto lens, a visual navigator, delves into scenes with a telescopic precision that adds depth to the visual odyssey.

In the visual arts showdown between the Galaxy S24 Ultra and iPhone 15 Pro Max, nuances become the battleground. The Galaxy S24 Ultra, armed with a 200-megapixel primary sensor and a dual telephoto ensemble, aims for pixel-rich magnificence. The iPhone 15 Pro Max, with its 48-megapixel primary sensor and periscope telephoto, pursues a visual odyssey painted with Apple's precision.

The Galaxy S24 Ultra, elevating the visual spectacle, introduces Nidography Zoom into the lexicon of smartphone photography. An innovation that transcends traditional zoom boundaries, Nidography Zoom becomes a quantum leap in visual storytelling. The Galaxy S24 Ultra, with its 100x space Zoom, invites users into a realm where details unfold with a clarity that defies conventional limits.

As the curtain rises on videography, the Galaxy S24 Ultra performs a ballet in 8K, recording scenes with a cinematic finesse at up to 60 frames per second. In contrast, the iPhone 15 Pro Max, limited to 4K recording at 60 frames per second, offers a visual narrative that, while commendable, encounters the spatial boundaries set by its resolution.

The Galaxy S24 Ultra introduces a symphony of High Dynamic Range (HDR) in 12-bit magnificence. A visual crescendo that transcends the conventional 10-bit HDR, the Galaxy S24 Ultra invites users into a realm where colors and contrasts become a palette of 68 billion possibilities. The iPhone 15 Pro Max, with its 10-bit HDR, offers a commendable performance, but the 12-bit HDR of the Galaxy S24 Ultra raises the bar in the visual symphony.

In the final act of this visual odyssey, the verdict is one of diversity. The Galaxy S24 Ultra and iPhone 15 Pro Max, each a virtuoso in the photographic arts, redefine smartphone photography not as a competition but as a symphony of visual epics. The nuances, whether in pixel-rich landscapes or telescopic details, become strokes in the canvas of user experiences. As users traverse the visual realms painted by these devices, the Galaxy S24 Ultra and iPhone 15 Pro Max, in their diversity, contribute to the evolving tapestry of smartphone photography excellence.

The Galaxy s24 Ultra's advanced camera features and improvements

The Samsung Galaxy s24 Ultra takes a quantum leap in the realm of smartphone photography, boasting a formidable quad rear camera setup that pushes the boundaries of what's possible. At its core is a groundbreaking 200-megapixel primary sensor, adorned with optical image stabilization (OIS) and a wide f/1.7 aperture.

This sensor forms the backbone of the camera system, capturing intricate details with unparalleled clarity.

Accompanying this photographic powerhouse is a dual telephoto sensor setup, demonstrating Samsung's commitment to versatility. The first telephoto lens is a 50-megapixel quad-pixel autofocus sensor, featuring OIS and an impressive 5x optical zoom capability with an f/3.4 aperture. This capability allows users to get closer to their subjects without compromising image quality.

The second telephoto lens is a 10-megapixel sensor supported by OIS, offering a 3x optical zoom and an f/2.4 aperture. Together, these telephoto lenses ensure that users can capture stunning shots, whether it's a distant landscape or a detailed close-up.

Complementing the telephoto prowess is a 12-megapixel ultrawide-angle sensor, providing a broad 120° field of view with an f/2.2 aperture. This sensor opens up creative possibilities, allowing users to experiment with different perspectives and capture expansive scenes in all their glory.

The front-facing camera of the Galaxy s24 Ultra is no slouch either. With a 12-megapixel sensor and an f/2.2 aperture, it ensures that your selfies are as sharp and vibrant as your rear camera shots.

However, the true magic lies not just in the hardware but in the advanced features that accompany this camera setup. Samsung brings to the table a host of cutting-edge functionalities, including Nidography Zoom for photos, AI multiframe processing across all zoom ranges, and deep learning-based super resolution. These features collectively elevate the camera experience, ensuring that every shot is a masterpiece.

Whether you're a photography enthusiast or a casual user, the Galaxy s24 Ultra's camera system is engineered to meet and exceed expectations. It's not just about the megapixels; it's about a harmonious fusion of hardware and software that transforms your moments into visual treasures. The Galaxy s24 Ultra is not merely a smartphone; it's a sophisticated imaging tool that empowers you to explore the boundaries of mobile photography.

Compare photo and video capabilities, including zoom, low-light performance, and AI features

In the dynamic realm of smartphone photography and videography, the Samsung Galaxy s24 Ultra and the iPhone 15 Pro Max engage in a fierce competition, each vying for the title of the ultimate visual storyteller. Let's delve into a comprehensive comparison of their photo and video capabilities, exploring zoom, low-light performance, and the prowess of AI features.

Zoom Capabilities:

The Galaxy s24 Ultra takes a quantum leap with its revolutionary Nidography Zoom, a feature that transcends conventional zoom capabilities. Sporting an impressive 100x Space Zoom, this smartphone allows users to bring the farthest subjects right into focus with astonishing detail. The dual telephoto lenses, featuring 5x and 3x optical zoom capabilities, ensure that users can effortlessly capture distant scenes without compromising image quality.

On the other side of the ring, the iPhone 15 Pro Max adopts a more conservative approach with a 5x optical zoom on its Periscope telephoto lens. While not reaching the astronomical heights of the Galaxy s24

Ultra, it still offers users a respectable zoom range for various shooting scenarios.

Low-Light Performance:

When the lights dim, the true capabilities of a smartphone camera shine through. The Galaxy s24 Ultra, equipped with advanced low-light optimization algorithms, showcases its prowess in challenging lighting conditions. The larger pixels on the primary sensor, coupled with sophisticated image processing, ensure that even in the darkest environments, your shots retain clarity, detail, and minimal noise.

The iPhone 15 Pro Max, no stranger to low-light photography, employs a combination of computational photography and its Night mode to capture stunning images in challenging conditions. While not matching the sheer megapixel count of its competitor, the iPhone excels in leveraging its sensor and software for impressive low-light results.

AI Features:

Both contenders bring Artificial Intelligence (AI) into the photographic arena, aiming to enhance user experience and image quality. The Galaxy s24 Ultra introduces AI multiframe processing across all zoom ranges, ensuring that every shot is a composition of intelligently captured frames. Deep learning-based super resolution takes image quality to new heights, pushing the boundaries of what a smartphone camera can achieve.

The iPhone 15 Pro Max, with its longstanding commitment to computational photography, employs AI to optimize various aspects of image capture. From Smart HDR to advanced noise reduction, Apple's AI algorithms work seamlessly to deliver visually stunning results.

Video Capabilities:

In the realm of videography, the Galaxy s24 Ultra stands out with its ability to record 8K videos at up to 60 frames per second. The Nidography Video feature brings the power of advanced zooming to video recording, allowing users to explore new cinematic possibilities.

The iPhone 15 Pro Max, while limited to 4K recording at 60 frames per second, delivers exceptional video quality. Apple's focus on color accuracy, dynamic range, and cinematic stabilization ensures that your videos are not just recordings but immersive visual experiences.

In the epic showdown of photo and video capabilities, both the Galaxy s24 Ultra and iPhone 15 Pro Max bring their A-game, catering to different preferences and shooting styles. Whether you prioritize unmatched zoom capabilities, superior low-light performance, or cutting-edge AI features, these smartphones have set the stage for a new era in mobile photography and videography.

Chapter 6:
Battery Battle

As we venture into the heart of these technological marvels, the discussion naturally gravitates towards a fundamental aspect of any mobile device—the battery. Both the Samsung Galaxy s24 Ultra and the iPhone 15 Pro Max come equipped with formidable power sources, each with its own set of specifications and charging capabilities.

Powering the Galaxy s24 Ultra is a robust 5,000 mAh battery unit, a continuation of the substantial power reservoir seen in its predecessor, the Galaxy s23 Ultra. This energy powerhouse ensures that users can navigate a day filled with calls, messages, multimedia consumption, and productivity without constantly worrying about running out of juice.

When it comes to replenishing this substantial battery, Samsung provides users with a 45 Watts fast charging solution. This feature enables a swift and efficient charging experience, allowing you to get back to your adventures with minimal downtime. However, it's essential to consider the overall power consumption, especially with the introduction of the Snapdragon 8 Gen 3 chipset, which, while enhancing performance, may impact battery efficiency.

On the Apple front, the iPhone 15 Pro Max is equipped with a slightly smaller 4,441 mAh battery unit. Apple, known for its optimization prowess in both hardware and software, ensures that this battery complements the device's overall efficiency.

While the numerical difference in capacity might not be vast, Apple's integration of power-saving features ensures a commendable balance between performance and battery life.

In terms of charging speeds, the iPhone 15 Pro Max offers a maximum of 30 Watts with its fast charging capability. Apple's focus on a more conservative approach to charging speeds is in line with its commitment to device longevity and overall user experience.

While the Galaxy s24 Ultra boasts a larger battery capacity and faster charging speeds on paper, it's crucial to consider the holistic efficiency, as the Snapdragon 8 Gen 3 chipset's performance demands might impact real-world battery life. On the other hand, the iPhone 15 Pro Max, while having a slightly smaller battery and a slower charging speed, benefits from Apple's meticulous optimization, offering a reliable and consistent user experience.

Ultimately, the choice between these devices depends on your preferences and usage patterns. Whether you prioritize a larger battery for extended usage or a meticulously optimized system that balances performance and efficiency, both smartphones cater to the diverse needs of modern users, ensuring that your device stays powered throughout your daily adventures.

The impact of the processors on overall battery life

The battle of processors in the Samsung Galaxy s24 Ultra, armed with the Snapdragon 8 Gen 3, and the iPhone 15 Pro Max, boasting the A17 Pro, not only defines their performance but significantly influences overall battery life.

The Galaxy s24 Ultra marks a significant leap in terms of performance, thanks to the Snapdragon 8 Gen 3 chipset. Engineered with the cutting-edge 4M ARM-based architecture, this powerhouse introduces a single core of the latest ARM Cortex X4-based Prime core, clocked at up to 3.3 GHz. This translates to impressive speed and responsiveness, especially in demanding tasks and resource-intensive applications.

However, the advancements in performance come at a cost—power consumption. Despite being a formidable performer, the Snapdragon 8 Gen 3 may draw more power, impacting overall battery efficiency. The intricacies of the architecture and the balance between high-performance and power efficiency cores play a crucial role in determining how effectively the Galaxy s24 Ultra manages its substantial 5,000 mAh battery.

On the Apple front, the iPhone 15 Pro Max relies on the A17 Pro processor, a powerhouse based on the 3M architecture. Apple's approach to processor design involves crafting their own cores based on the ARM architecture, showcasing years of expertise in delivering top-tier performance.

While the A17 Pro might not boast the same GHz figures as its Snapdragon counterpart, Apple has consistently proven its prowess in optimizing hardware and software. The result is a device that delivers exceptional single-core performance, maintaining a delicate balance between power and efficiency. This meticulous optimization contributes to extending the overall battery life of the iPhone 15 Pro Max.

In the relentless pursuit of performance, there's always a trade-off, especially concerning battery life. The Snapdragon 8 Gen 3's impressive multi-core performance puts the Galaxy s24 Ultra at the forefront of raw processing power. However, users must be mindful of the potential impact on battery life, especially with resource-intensive tasks.

On the flip side, Apple's A17 Pro, while slightly lagging in raw performance metrics, excels in single-core tasks and power efficiency. This optimized harmony between hardware and software ensures that the iPhone 15 Pro Max delivers a commendable battery life without compromising on performance.

Ultimately, the choice between these devices hinges on your priorities—whether you crave the bleeding-edge multi-core performance of the Snapdragon 8 Gen 3 or the meticulously tuned power efficiency of Apple's A17 Pro. It's a delicate dance between power and optimization, and both smartphones showcase the best of their respective ecosystems.

User's daily usage scenarios for predicting screen-on time

To predict the screen-on time for both the Samsung Galaxy s24 Ultra and the iPhone 15 Pro Max, we must delve into the intricacies of users' daily scenarios and how each device handles various usage patterns.

The Galaxy s24 Ultra, armed with the Snapdragon 8 Gen 3, is designed for users who demand peak performance across a spectrum of tasks. Whether you're engaging in resource-intensive gaming, multitasking with numerous applications, or unleashing the potential of the advanced camera system, the Galaxy s24 Ultra can handle it all.

For users who frequently engage in gaming or media consumption, the stunning QHD+ Dynamic AMOLED 2x display with a 120Hz refresh rate becomes a central player. While it delivers an immersive visual experience, it also requires a substantial amount of power. Additionally, the demands placed on the processor during intense gaming sessions or complex multitasking scenarios may impact overall battery life.

On the flip side, if your daily routine involves more casual tasks, such as browsing, social media, and occasional photography, the Galaxy s24 Ultra's advanced performance capabilities might not be fully utilized. In such scenarios, the device's power efficiency features and adaptive refresh rate can contribute to preserving battery life.

The iPhone 15 Pro Max, housing the A17 Pro, excels in delivering a seamless and efficient user experience. Apple's ecosystem optimization ensures that the device performs exceptionally well in everyday tasks, emphasizing the importance of single-core performance.

If your daily usage revolves around productivity, communication, and occasional media consumption, the iPhone

15 Pro Max is poised to offer a consistently smooth experience. The 120Hz Super Retina XDR OLED display, coupled with the efficiency of the A17 Pro, strikes a balance between visual brilliance and battery preservation.

Predicting screen-on time involves understanding the user's priorities and the nature of their interactions with the device. Both smartphones cater to diverse user profiles, from power users who demand the utmost in performance to individuals with more restrained usage patterns.

In scenarios where the demands on processing power are high, such as gaming or content creation, the Galaxy s24 Ultra's robust hardware might result in slightly shorter screen-on times. On the other hand, the iPhone 15 Pro Max's emphasis on efficiency and optimization might lead to more consistent screen-on times across various usage scenarios.

Ultimately, the choice between the Galaxy s24 Ultra and iPhone 15 Pro Max is not just about raw specifications but about aligning the device's capabilities with your specific daily needs. It's a nuanced decision that revolves around finding the right balance between performance and efficiency based on your unique usage patterns.

Chapter 7:
Software Symphony

The realm of smartphones is not solely defined by cutting-edge hardware and innovative features; it is equally influenced by the longevity and relevance of software support. Both Samsung and Apple understand the importance of providing users with consistent updates to enhance security, introduce new features, and ensure a seamless experience. Let's delve into the software support commitments from these tech giants.

With the introduction of the Galaxy s24 Ultra, Samsung has taken a bold step in the realm of software support. The company has committed to providing an impressive seven years of software updates for the Galaxy s24 Ultra. This goes beyond routine security patches, extending to major operating system upgrades. It's a move that aligns with Samsung's recognition of the evolving nature of technology and the desire to offer users a device that remains relevant for an extended period.

This commitment encompasses a promise to deliver the latest Android versions, ensuring that users can enjoy the latest features and optimizations even as the mobile landscape evolves. Samsung's One UI, known for its user-friendly interface and customization options, will continue to evolve alongside Android updates, enhancing the overall user experience.

Apple, a trailblazer in the domain of software support, has long set the gold standard for other manufacturers. The iPhone 15 Pro Max, like its predecessors, benefits from Apple's exceptional commitment to software updates. Apple typically provides iOS updates to its devices for a significant number of years.

In the case of the iPhone 15 Pro Max, users can expect to receive not only routine security updates but also major iOS upgrades for several years. This ensures that Apple device owners consistently enjoy the latest iOS features, security enhancements, and improvements in overall performance.

The prolonged software support from both Samsung and Apple translates into a more significant investment for users. Owning a flagship device like the Galaxy s24 Ultra or iPhone 15 Pro Max becomes a long-term commitment with the assurance of a device that remains current in terms of both hardware and software.

Samsung's shift towards an extended software support window is a noteworthy move that brings its flagship devices closer to Apple's renowned commitment. Users now have the confidence that their premium devices will not become outdated quickly, making the choice between the Galaxy s24 Ultra and iPhone 15 Pro Max not just a matter of hardware preferences but a consideration of the long-term software experience.

In the ever-evolving landscape of mobile technology, where new features and security measures are continually introduced, both

Samsung and Apple's dedication to extended software support ensures that users can extract maximum value from their flagship devices over an extended period. Whether you lean towards the Android ecosystem with the Galaxy s24 Ultra or the iOS realm with the iPhone 15 Pro Max, the promise of prolonged software updates adds a layer of assurance to your smartphone investment.

The seven years of software update support for the Galaxy s24 Ultra

Samsung has made a resounding statement in the tech arena by elevating the standard for software support with the Galaxy s24 Ultra. A flagship device that not only dazzles with its cutting-edge hardware but also stands as a testament to Samsung's commitment to user satisfaction over an extended period. The key highlight? A remarkable seven years of promised software update support.

In an industry where technological advancements seem to sprint forward, Samsung has chosen to redefine the narrative of smartphone longevity. The Galaxy s24 Ultra, crowned with the promise of seven years of software updates, signifies more than just routine patches and security enhancements. It symbolizes a pledge to keep the device relevant, adaptive, and feature-rich throughout its lifecycle.

This bold move from Samsung resonates with the dynamic nature of the tech landscape. Users, often faced with the dilemma of device obsolescence, can now revel in the assurance that their Galaxy s24 Ultra will evolve with time. Major Android updates, each bringing a bouquet of new features, optimizations, and enhancements, will continue to grace this flagship device for an impressive span.

This commitment aligns with Samsung's vision of not just delivering a product but fostering an enduring relationship with users. The seven years of software support for the Galaxy s24 Ultra means that users won't be left behind in the fast-paced race of technological innovation. It's an invitation to partake in the future of mobile technology without the anxiety of premature obsolescence.

The implications of this extended software support are profound. Users investing in the Galaxy s24 Ultra aren't merely getting a device for the present; they're securing a ticket to a future where their smartphone experience evolves in tandem with the ever-changing tech landscape. It's a move that sets a new benchmark in an industry where longevity has often been associated with incremental compromises.

As users navigate the digital landscape, the Galaxy s24 Ultra stands tall as a beacon of sustained innovation. The seven years of software updates are not just a numerical feat; they represent a paradigm shift in how we perceive the lifecycle of flagship smartphones. Samsung, with the Galaxy s24

Ultra, has not just raised the bar; it has redefined the rules of the game, ensuring that users can embrace the future without bidding farewell to the present. It's not just a device; it's a testament to Samsung's commitment to a journey that spans seven years of technological excellence.

The user experience, AI features, and software integration on both devices

In the intricate dance of technology and user interaction, both the Samsung Galaxy s24 Ultra and the iPhone 15 Pro Max emerge as maestros, each conducting a symphony of features, AI capabilities, and software integration to deliver an unparalleled user experience.

The Samsung Galaxy s24 Ultra steps onto the stage with a plethora of AI features that not only enhance daily interactions but also redefine what a smartphone can achieve. Live translation of calls, an AI note assistant, and the groundbreaking Nidography Zoom are just glimpses into the AI-powered universe that the Galaxy s24 Ultra offers. It's not just about having a powerful device; it's about having an intelligent companion that understands and adapts to your needs seamlessly.

One of the standout features is the Nidography Zoom, a testament to Samsung's commitment to pushing the boundaries of what's possible in mobile photography. This AI-powered zoom technology goes beyond conventional limits, offering users the ability to zoom in with astounding clarity across various ranges. It's not just about capturing a moment; it's about capturing it with unprecedented detail and precision.

The AI note assistant takes productivity to new heights, making the Galaxy s24 Ultra more than just a communication device. It becomes a dynamic tool for creativity, organization, and expression. Whether it's jotting down ideas, transcribing notes, or even translating text, the AI note assistant is a digital companion that evolves with you.

Switching gears to the iPhone 15 Pro Max, Apple brings its signature blend of intuitive user experience and seamless software integration to the forefront. The iOS ecosystem has long been celebrated for its simplicity and uniformity, creating an environment where users can navigate effortlessly. The A17 Pro chipset, Apple's custom creation, ensures that every interaction is swift, responsive, and tailored for optimal performance.

While Samsung introduces users to the boundless possibilities of AI, Apple relies on its cohesive ecosystem to deliver a streamlined experience. Siri, Apple's virtual assistant, takes center stage, providing users with a hands-free means of navigating their devices. From setting reminders to sending messages, Siri is the voice-activated bridge between user intent and device execution.

Both devices, in their own way, exemplify the marriage of hardware and software to create an immersive user experience. The Galaxy s24 Ultra, with its AI-centric approach, invites users into a world of endless possibilities. On the other hand, the iPhone 15 Pro Max, anchored in the iOS ecosystem, delivers a user experience that seamlessly integrates across Apple devices.

In the grand tapestry of user-centric features, AI innovations, and software integration, the Galaxy s24 Ultra and iPhone 15 Pro Max emerge as champions, each offering a unique journey through the landscape of modern technology. It's a tale of two titans, each vying for the user's heart by weaving a narrative of innovation, intelligence, and an experience that transcends the ordinary.

Chapter 8:

The Verdict

The strengths and weaknesses of each smartphone

The Samsung Galaxy s24 Ultra and iPhone 15 Pro Max, two behemoths in the smartphone arena, each bring a unique set of strengths and, inevitably, a few areas where they tread cautiously.

Samsung Galaxy s24 Ultra

Strengths:

1. Revolutionary Camera System: The Galaxy s24 Ultra sets a new standard with its 200-megapixel primary sensor, backed by a versatile dual telephoto setup and advanced AI features like Nidography Zoom.

2. Stunning Display: The QHD+ Dynamic AMOLED 2x display is a visual feast, offering crisp details, vibrant colors, and a smooth 120Hz refresh rate.

3. AI-Powered Features: The AI note assistant, live translation, and Nidography Zoom showcase Samsung's commitment to a smart and intuitive user experience.

4. Generous Battery: Despite a power-hungry processor, the 5,000mAh battery provides ample juice for daily use.

Weaknesses:

1. Weight: Weighing in at 232g, the Galaxy s24 Ultra might feel a bit hefty for some users.

2. Charging Speed: While offering 45W fast charging, it faces stiff competition from

other brands pushing higher charging speeds.

iPhone 15 Pro Max

Strengths:

1. Optimized Ecosystem: Apple's iOS ecosystem ensures seamless integration across devices, delivering a consistent and user-friendly experience.
2. A17 Pro Chipset: Apple's custom processor provides top-tier performance and power efficiency, maintaining a lead in single-core benchmarks.
3. Well-Optimized Software: iOS updates are promptly available, ensuring a long-lasting and consistent software experience.

4. Reliable Camera System: While not as groundbreaking as the Galaxy s24 Ultra, the iPhone's camera system delivers reliable and high-quality results.

Weaknesses:

1. Limited Zoom Capability: The iPhone 15 Pro Max lags behind in the zoom department, with a 5x optical zoom compared to the Galaxy s24 Ultra's 10x.
2. Battery Capacity: With a slightly smaller battery at 4441mAh, it may not match the Galaxy s24 Ultra in prolonged usage scenarios.

In this clash of titans, the Galaxy s24 Ultra shines with its innovative camera capabilities and AI-driven features, while the iPhone 15 Pro Max leverages its optimized ecosystem and robust performance. Each device caters to a specific user preference, offering a nuanced choice in the diverse landscape of flagship smartphones.

Final recommendation based on user preferences and priorities

In the grand arena of smartphone supremacy, choosing between the Samsung Galaxy s24 Ultra and the iPhone 15 Pro Max ultimately boils down to your individual preferences and priorities.

Choose the Samsung Galaxy s24 Ultra if:

- Photography is Your Passion: If you're captivated by the art of photography and desire a smartphone that pushes the boundaries, the Galaxy s24 Ultra's groundbreaking 200-megapixel camera and innovative features make it an ideal companion.

- Display Brilliance Matters: For those who revel in a visual extravaganza, the Galaxy s24 Ultra's QHD+ Dynamic AMOLED 2x display, with its vibrant colors, crisp details, and smooth 120Hz refresh rate, promises an immersive viewing experience.

- AI-Powered Convenience: Embrace the future with Samsung's AI features, from live translation to Nidography Zoom, enhancing your daily interactions and making your smartphone an intelligent companion.

- Extended Software Support: The promise of seven years of software updates positions the Galaxy s24 Ultra as a long-term investment, ensuring your device stays current with the latest features and security patches.

Opt for the iPhone 15 Pro Max if:

- Ecosystem Consistency: If you're already entrenched in the Apple ecosystem with other devices, the iPhone 15 Pro Max seamlessly integrates into the ecosystem, providing a consistent and streamlined user experience.

- Top-Tier Performance: Apple's A17 Pro chipset ensures top-tier performance, particularly in single-core tasks. If you prioritize swift and responsive device performance, the iPhone has the edge.

- Reliability in Camera and Software: While not as revolutionary as its counterpart, the iPhone's camera system is reliable and delivers high-quality results. Additionally, Apple's well-optimized iOS ensures a stable and consistent software experience.

- Balanced Approach: If you seek a balanced approach between performance, reliability, and a well-integrated ecosystem, the iPhone 15 Pro Max caters to those who value a harmonious blend of features.

Ultimately, whether you embark on the Samsung or Apple journey, both devices are technological marvels, each with its unique strengths. Let your priorities guide you through this digital odyssey, and may your chosen smartphone be the perfect companion in your daily adventures.

Conclusion

In the fast-paced realm of ultra-flagship smartphones, the Samsung Galaxy s24 Ultra and the iPhone 15 Pro Max stand as epitomes of technological brilliance. As we conclude this exploration into the intricacies of these devices, it's evident that the choice between them is not a one-size-fits-all decision. Rather, it's a reflection of your individual needs, desires, and the technological journey you envision.

The Samsung Galaxy s24 Ultra, with its revolutionary 200-megapixel camera, QHD+ Dynamic AMOLED 2x display, and seven years of software support, charts a course into the future of smartphone innovation. Samsung's commitment to AI features and cutting-edge hardware positions the Galaxy s24 Ultra as a beacon of possibilities.

On the other hand, the iPhone 15 Pro Max, with its seamless integration into the Apple ecosystem, powerful A17 Pro chipset, and the reliability of iOS, offers a different yet equally compelling narrative. For those entrenched in the Apple universe, it's a continuation of a familiar and well-crafted experience.

As readers navigate the intricate landscape of specifications and features, the emphasis remains on making an informed decision aligned with individual preferences. The dynamics of technology are ever-evolving, and the competition between giants like

Samsung and Apple fuels a perpetual cycle of innovation.

In this era of constant progress, where every flagship release brings forth new capabilities and refinements, the reader is encouraged to stay attuned to their specific needs. The smartphone you choose is not merely a device; it's a companion on your journey, a portal to connectivity, creativity, and convenience.

So, as you embark on the quest for your next ultra-flagship smartphone, let your needs guide you, and may your chosen device be a testament to the exciting convergence of technology and personal preference. The future is undeniably promising, and your smartphone is a gateway to the boundless possibilities that lie ahead. Choose wisely, and may your digital adventures be extraordinary.